THE MOST ENTERTAINING CURE-ALL SINCE THE PILL!

It's just what the doctor ordered! So, take two guffaws and call him in the morning—because laughter is the drug we all need more of. It oxygenates the brain, reduces stress, and *really* impresses the boss on Monday mornings. So take a tip from Doctor Lanigan: when you're suffering from acute job-itis and inflammation of the taxes, this book is the remedy—and the prognosis is laughter!

St. Martin's Paperbacks Titles by Suds Lanigan

A MAN WALKED INTO A BAR
A MINISTER, A RABBI AND A PRIEST . . .
WHAT'S UP, DOC?

St. Martin's Paperbacks titles are available at quantity discounts for sales promotions, premiums or fund raising. Special books or book excerpts can also be created to fit specific needs.

For information write to special sales manager, St. Martin's Press, 175 Fifth Avenue, New York, N.Y. 10010.

WHAT'S UP, DOC?

Hilarious, ribald and tasteless jokes about nurses, doctors, psychiatrists, hospitals, dentists and patients

SUDS LANIGAN

ST. MARTIN'S PAPERBACKS

NOTE: If you purchased this book without a cover you should be aware that this book is stolen property. It was reported as 'unsold and destroyed' to the publisher, and neither the author nor the publisher has received any payment for this 'stripped book'.

WHAT'S UP, DOC?

Copyright © 1991 by James Charlton Associates.

All rights reserved. No part of this book may be used or reproduced in any manner whatsoever without written permission except in the case of brief quotations embodied in critical articles or reviews. For information address St. Martin's Press, 175 Fifth Avenue, New York, N.Y. 10010.

ISBN: 0-312-92201-9

Printed in the United States of America

St. Martin's Paperbacks edition/October 1991

10 9 8 7 6 5 4 3 2 1

Mr. Jackson was having some troubling pains in his chest. Worried that he might have cancer, he went to his family doctor. After an initial series of examinations, the family doctor was still perplexed, and recommended a specialist at the hospital. The specialist was consulted and performed further tests on Mr. Jackson. Finally, the doctor sat his patient down.

"I'm sorry to tell you this, Mr. Jackson, but you seem to have contracted an incurable disease. I'd give you inside of three months to live."

Jackson slumped back in his chair. "Doctor, that's just not fair. I'm still a young man, I have a family, a wife and two young children to support. Mortgage payments, school. Heck,

I can't even come up with enough money to pay you in three months."

The doctor thought for a moment. "Okay, then I'll give you six months to live."

Mr. Rasmussen returned from an extended trip and, not feeling well, visited his doctor. The doctor performed a series of tests on him and the patient was instructed to return in a few days for the results.

When the man returned the doctor sat him down. "Mr. Rasmussen, I have some bad news for you. The tests show that you have syphillis, gonorrhea, AIDS and leprosy."

Rasmussen was shocked and slumped down in his chair. "Doctor, what do you recommend?"

The doctor said, "Well, we have an isolated wing in the hospital and a room has been prepared for you. And we have a special diet for you of flounder and pancakes."

"Flounder and pancakes?" gasped Mr. Rasmussen. "Will that help?"

"No," replied the doctor, "but it's the only thing we can slide under the door."

WHAT'S UP, DOC?

Roscoe and his pregnant wife were ranchers in Wyoming and lived miles from the nearest town. One evening, while his wife and he were finishing up in the barn, the labor pains started. Collapsing on a bale of hay, Roscoe's wife cried out, "I can't move. Call the doctor in Sheridan. The baby's coming!"

Roscoe raced to the house and dialed the doctor, who assured him he would be there in twenty minutes and that Roscoe should keep his wife warm and not try and move her. Roscoe rushed back to the barn and, minutes later, the doctor arrived. Directing Roscoe to hold a light over the prostrate woman, the doctor swiftly performed his ministrations.

"Hold the light a little closer now, Roscoe," the doctor ordered. "There! I'd like to congratulate you. You're the father of a beautiful baby boy!"

"Thank you so much, doctor," Roscoe gasped emotionally.

"Wait a minute, hold the light a little closer again," said the doctor. "Well, well! Now you're the father of *two* brand-new baby boys." The doctor proudly held up the latest arrival.

"Thank you so much, doctor," said Roscoe, backing away to a corner of the barn.

"Not so fast, Roscoe, bring the light a little closer. Make that *three* boys!" the doctor said triumphantly, as he pulled another little head through.

"Well, Doc, thanks, I guess," Roscoe began to turn the light out.

"Wait a minute, Roscoe, bring the lamp back over," the doctor motioned.

"Excuse me, doctor," Roscoe demurred, "but don't you think it might be the light that keeps attracting them?"

DUE TO OVERCROWDING in the restaurant, an elderly gentleman was forced to share his table with a quiet man in a dark suit. The senior citizen ordered a large sirloin, and when the waiter returned with it, the man dug around in his bag looking for something. "Oh, no," he said disgustedly. "I seem to have forgotten my dentures, and this delicious steak will go to waste."

Without a word, the other man rummaged through a leather valise next to him and pulled out a set of dentures. The older man, eager to eat the now-cooling steak, gratefully took the dentures and fit them in his mouth —but, alas, found that they were too small.

"Thanks, mister, it was a good try," he said regretfully. "I've got a hard mouth to fit for dentures."

His table companion nodded at the elderly gentleman and without a word searched through his bag again. This time he produced a pair that fit perfectly and the octogenarian eagerly went at his meal.

When he had finished the steak, the man leaned back and sighed contentedly, "Thanks a lot, doctor. You know, you're the first person I've met who has given me an exact match for dentures. Where is your dentist's office and when can I get an appointment?"

"Oh well, I'm afraid you can't get an appointment," the man replied, "I'm not a dentist. I'm a mortician."

A WOMAN IN HER MID 40S walked into her Doctor's office blushing a little. "Doctor," said the woman, "I'm having a well, a difficulty, and ah—"

The doctor, sensing something was bothering the woman, replied, "Please dear, I'm a doctor. I've heard far worse, no doubt, than you can tell me."

The woman continued. "Well, it started a few days ago. I went to go to the bathroom, and to my shock, pennies started coming out. But I didn't really worry, I figured it would stop."

"I understand. Go on," the doctor said.

"To my surprise, when I went to the bathroom the next day, painfully enough, nickels started coming out. This was very uncomfortable."

"Of course it was," nodded the doctor.

"The next day I went to the bathroom, and out came a bunch of shiny dimes. At this point, I was afraid of what would happen the next day."

"And what did happen?" asked the doctor.

"As I predicted, quarters came out. Doctor, what do you make of all this?"

The doctor smiled gently at the woman. "It's no problem, Mrs. Kent. You're just going through the change."

WHAT'S UP, DOC?

THE DOCTOR ATTENDED a conference in Europe, and brought his secretary to organize his appointments. Their plane arrived late and they reached the hotel to find that they were assigned just one room. Having to get up early the next day, they took it.

It was cold that night, as they both slipped under the covers. The secretary turned to the doctor. "Doctor, would you mind slipping out of bed to close the window?"

The doctor replied, "Would you like to pretend that you are my wife tonight?"

"Oh yes!" cried the secretary. "I was hoping you would ask me!"

"Good," said the doctor turning over. "Then close the window yourself!"

A MAN RUSHED into the doctor's office and pleaded, "Doctor, doctor, I have a terrible ringing in my ears! You have to do something!"

"How long has this been going on?" inquired the doctor.

"At least a year," the man replied. "I've been to specialists all over the country and I've taken every pill they prescribed and followed every program they've given me. Nothing worked."

"It's a real coincidence," said the doctor, "but I had the same trouble!"

"What did you do?" asked the man, clutching the doctor's arm.

"I spent three months with my head between my wife's legs and it cured me," answered the doctor. "Why don't you try it?"

Three months later the man, looking much more relaxed, came back in the office.

"How is everything?" asked the doctor.

"Great, the ringing in my ears is gone. I'm completely back to normal," answered the man. "And by the way, I really like your house."

A YOUNG WOMAN wasn't feeling well, and asked one of her co-workers to recommend a physician.

"I know a great one in the city, but he is very expensive. Five hundred dollars for the first visit, and one hundred dollars for each one after that."

The woman went to the doctor's office and,

trying to save a little money, cheerily announced, "I'm back!"

Not fooled for a second, the doctor quickly examined her and said, "Very good, just continue the treatment I prescribed on your last visit."

THE DOCTOR WAS MAKING his rounds and walked into the semi-private room in the hospital to examine old Mrs. Waxman. After the exam in his best professional voice, he said smoothly, "You are coughing much more easily this morning."

"I should," snapped the patient. "I've been practicing all night."

THE TWO INTERNS were in the emergency ward when a new patient was brought in and put on the table. He was unconscious and feverish and the interns had to put their hands under him to lift him. By accident, they grabbed each other's hand.

"Nothing serious," said the first intern.

"He's probably drunk," said the second.

THE HUSBAND AND WIFE were in the waiting room when the doctor came out to see them.

"And what seems to be the problem with your husband, Mrs. Taylor?" asked the doctor.

The woman answered. "His problem seems to be that he's constantly worried about money."

"Ah," said the doctor, "I think we can relieve him of that."

THE INFIRMARY DOCTOR was examining the college student and asked him to breathe in and out while he listened with a stethoscope.

"I see you've had some problems with Angina Pectoris," observed the doctor.

WHAT'S UP, DOC?

"You're right, doctor," answered the young man. "But that wasn't her name."

THE MAN WALKED INTO THE DOCTOR'S OFFICE for a follow-up visit. The doctor came out to see him and said, "Of course you followed the prescription I gave you."

"I certainly didn't, Doctor," protested the patient. "If I had I'd have broken my neck!"

"Broken your neck?" questioned the doctor.

"Yeah, I threw your prescription out my fifth floor window."

MRS. WINSTON CALLED as soon as she received the doctor's bill.

"I think you've overcharged on this bill. My son Jimmy only had the flu."

"That's true," agreed the nurse. "But you brought him in here nearly a dozen times."

"I know. But you forget he infected the whole school."

THE YOUNG WOMAN LOOKED UP from her hospital bed at the handsome doctor and said breathlessly, "They tell me, doctor, that you're a real lady killer."

The doctor smiled, "Oh no, I can assure you —I make no distinction between the sexes."

AFTER THREE DAYS IN A COMA the man finally regained consciousness. He opened his eyes to find the doctor taking his pulse.

"You were on death's doorstep, Mr. Winters," said the doctor gravely. "It's only your strong constitution that has pulled you through."

"I just hope you remember that, Doctor, when you send me your bill."

WHAT'S UP, DOC?

THE YOUNG MAN had been in the hospital for nearly a month and in that time had grown very fond of the pretty nurse in attendance. She had even responded a bit and, as part of his therapy, had kissed him several times. The young man was almost well enough to go home, and this particular morning he grabbed the nurse's hand as she stood next to his bed.

"I'm desperately in love with you," he gasped. "I don't want to get well."

"Don't worry, you won't," said the nurse sweetly. "Your doctor's in love with me and he saw you kissing me yesterday."

THE PATIENT SAT IN THE CHAIR as the dentist was busy adjusting his tools.

"I'll be with you in a minute," the dentist said. "I must have my drill first."

The patient looked up in astonishment. "Can't you pull a tooth without a rehearsal?"

Suds Lanigan

A Frenchman, an Englishman and an Israeli were working on a power plant in the middle of the desert when they were accidentally exposed to a lethal dosage of radiation. The doctor examined them and mournfully shook his head. The three men only had a short time to live and the doctor, in an effort to make their final time as pleasant as possible, granted them each one last wish.

The Frenchman wished to spend his last night with the most beautiful woman in the world. The Englishman asked for an audience with the Queen. The Israeli wanted to see another doctor.

Mrs. Zuckerman went to see the doctor about her husband's problem. "Doctor," she started, "my husband, Mort, keeps me awake all the time. Every night he gets up and sleepwalks. It's driving me crazy. Is there anything I can do about it?"

WHAT'S UP, DOC?

The Doctor thought for a moment before replying.

"There's one thing I can recommend to cure him of sleepwalking. Try putting a large pan of water on the floor beside his bed. Then when he sleepwalks, he'll step in it and it'll wake him up."

Mrs. Zuckerman rushed home to put the doctor's advice into action. But the very next day she was back in the doctor's office.

"Well, Mrs. Zuckerman, did you take my advice and put the pan of water by the side of the bed?"

She nodded her head.

"And did it cure him?"

"Yes," she said, "and it cured me of putting a pan of water by his bed."

THE DENTIST LEANED OVER the patient in the chair.

"Open wider."

"Wider."

"Wider."

Suddenly the patient sat up. "Listen, if you're going to get in, I'm getting out!"

The elderly patient looked up at the doctor and asked, "Doctor, how long am I going to live?"

"Don't worry," the doctor replied, "you should live to be eighty."

"I *am* eighty," he answered.

"See? What'd I tell you?"

The archbishop was sitting in the waiting room when a red-faced and crying nun ran by him from the doctor's inner office. The angry bishop charged into the office and demanded to know what the doctor had said.

"I told her she was pregnant," answered the doctor.

"It is certainly not true. Why would you possibly tell her something like that?" demanded the archbishop.

"Well," replied the doctor, "it cured her hiccups!"

WHAT'S UP, DOC?

DURING HIS ANNUAL PHYSICAL, the doctor asked Mr. Smith to lean out the window and stick out his tongue.

"You ask me to do that every year, and I never know why."

"Oh, there's no medical reason," assured the doctor. "I just don't like my neighbors."

AT A COCKTAIL PARTY, the lawyer was getting annoyed at the number of people who kept asking for free advice. He asked his doctor friend if he had the same problem.

"All the time," agreed the doctor.

"Well, don't you get tired of it? What do you do?" asked the lawyer.

"It's very simple, and I think it will work for you," said the doctor. "When they ask for advice, just tell them to undress!"

"Doctor! Doctor! Will I be able to read after I get these glasses?"

"Oh certainly," replied the doctor.

"Great! I could never read before."

A NINETY-ONE-YEAR-OLD MAN and his eighty-five-year-old wife went to the doctor for a physical.

"This is amazing," said the doctor, "This is amazing. You are both in perfect health!"

"Good," replied the man. "Now we can get a divorce."

"A divorce!" exclaimed the doctor. "After all these years, how could you get a divorce now?"

"Well, we wanted to wait until the children were dead."

WHAT'S UP, DOC?

AFTER A SERIES OF EXPENSIVE TESTS and examinations on Mr. Dunne, the doctor threw up his hands and explained, "I can do nothing for you. Your problem is hereditary."

"Then send the bill to my father," snapped the patient.

THE TRAVELING SALESMAN went to the doctor, complaining of fatigue. After a routine series of tests, the doctor said, "Well, the tests don't reveal anything, so let's take this from a new perspective. How often do you engage in sexual relations?"

"Three times a night on Monday, Wednesday, Friday, and Saturday," replied the salesman.

"Oh, that explains it," said the doctor, "I suggest you take a rest on Wednesday."

"Oh, I couldn't do that, Doctor. That's the only night of the week that I'm home."

SUDS LANIGAN

Bob was getting married on Saturday. However, the day before, he was in a car accident and tore a groin muscle right near his penis. His doctor said the only solution was to wear a splint made of four pieces of wood. Bob was heartbroken. "Doctor, tomorrow's my wedding night!" Nevertheless, he acceded to his doctor's wishes, and the splint was applied.

That night at the hotel, his new bride began to take off her clothes. As she dropped her slip to her waist, she smiled demurely. "Look at these, Bob. They have never been touched by a man before."

As she dropped her slip to the floor, she lowered her gaze. "And down here, Bob. This has never been seen by a man before."

At this point Bob dropped his robe and said, "You think that is impressive, look at this. Still in the original crate!"

The new bride went to a sex therapy specialist, complaining that she felt nothing during intercourse. After a series of tests, the doctor decided to try for himself. He instructed her to disrobe and to get on the table. And she willingly obliged. In preparation the doctor put

WHAT'S UP, DOC?

on a condom. After a few minutes of gentle thrusting, the doctor asked her if she felt anything.

"No, I'm sorry, I don't," replied the patient apologetically.

The doctor continued for a few more minutes, picking up the pace. Still the woman felt nothing. Now he went at a ferocious speed for about fifteen minutes. Exhausted, finally he had to stop.

Out of breath, he asked the woman, "Did you feel anything?"

"No, I feel terrible, but I didn't."

"Nothing? No sensation at all?"

The girl thought for a moment. "There was the smell of burning rubber!"

A MAN WENT TO HIS DOCTOR, complaining of severe groin cramps. After an exam, the doctor told the man that he was sexually frustrated, and suggested that the man hire a prostitute as a way of releasing his tension.

The man left the office and headed for the red light district. He explained his problem to a prostitute, and they went off to a hotel. Afterwards the man felt much better until the hooker said, "Okay, buddy, that's two hundred dollars."

"Two hundred dollars! You have got to be crazy! I told you this was medical!"

"Medical for you but it is still just business. I need two hundred dollars."

The man pulled out a business card. "All right, but you'll have to wait for my Blue Cross!"

AN EXPECTANT MOTHER asked her doctor, "Will my husband be allowed to stay in the delivery room during the birth?"

"Oh yes, of course. I think it is very important that the father be present."

"Oh no! I don't think we should let the father in. He and my husband don't get along too well!"

A CONCERNED WOMAN called the doctor and explained that her husband was very ill.

WHAT'S UP, DOC?

"I know this is a lot to ask, Doctor," said the woman, "but we live far from town and the car is broken and my husband is quite sick. Is it possible for you to come out here?"

"No problem," boomed the doctor, "I have another patient to visit in the neighborhood. I'll just kill two birds with one stone!"

WHILE WORKING with high-speed equipment, Tom accidentally got his fingers caught in an electric saw and managed to shave off all ten digits.

He rushed to the hospital where the doctor said, "It looks good, Tom. You got here fast enough that I think we can put your fingers back on!"

"But Doctor, I didn't bring them!"

"What?!" exclaimed the physician. "In these days of microsurgery and medical miracles you forgot the fingers?!"

"I didn't forget 'em, Doctor. I just couldn't pick them up!"

A famous surgeon was giving the commencement address to a graduating class of medical students. At the end of the speech, he conducted a question-and-answer session, and one of the students asked how he had become so successful at medicine.

"Well," he began, "when I started medical school, all I could think of was dancing. I would call girls constantly to go out and dance. Except that every time I did, my father wouldn't let me forget it. Eventually, every time I went towards the phone, he passed me a textbook. In the end, I forgot dancing and concentrated on my studies. I spent enough time at it that I graduated first in my class and became the success that I am today."

"Wow!" said one student to the other. "The story of one of the world's great doctors."

"No," corrected his classmate. "The story of one of the world's worst dancers."

WHAT'S UP, DOC?

Mike said to his psychiatrist, "I can't get over this feeling that I was supposed to be born as a dog."

"How long has this been going on?" asked the psychiatrist.

"Since I was a puppy!"

"Doctor! Doctor!" said the woman to her psychiatrist. "Everyone treats my husband like a parking meter!"

"Well, isn't he his own person? Why doesn't he speak up for himself?"

"He would, but his mouth is full of quarters!"

"Doctor! Doctor!" said the woman to her psychiatrist. "My husband thinks he's a refrigerator!"

"Why exactly does that bother you?"

"He sleeps with his mouth open and the light keeps me up!"

Ms. Jones was interviewing a man about to be released from a mental hospital after ten years of therapy.

"What do you think you'll do when you get out?" asked Ms. Jones.

"I think I may resume my law practice," said the patient, "or possibly finish my accounting degree. Then again, since I have a medical degree, I could pursue that. I could practice psychiatry and use all of the techniques that I have learned while I have been here."

Ms. Jones was impressed. "It sounds like you have a number of interesting choices."

"That's true. And if all else fails, I could be a tea kettle!"

Bubba was up for parole. In order to be considered, he had to pass an exam given by the prison psychiatrist. The doctor asked him, "Well, Bubba, what would you do if you were released today?"

Bubba looked around. "I'd get a slingshot and knock out all of the windows in this building!"

He was sent back to his cell. Six months later, he was sent to the psychiatrist again.

"Well, Bubba, what would you do if you were released today?"

"I'd go buy a new suit," replied Bubba.

"Much better," said the doctor. "And then what?"

"Then I'd call up the hottest blonde I know and take her to a motel!"

"Very normal, this is an encouraging improvement over our conversation six months ago. Then what would you do?"

"Then I'd make a slingshot out of her pantyhose, come back here, and knock out all of the windows in this building!"

THE DOCTOR ANSWERED THE PHONE and heard the familiar voice of a colleague on the other end of the line. "We need a fourth for poker," said the friend.

"I'll be right over," whispered the doctor.

As he was putting on his coat, his wife asked, "Is it serious?"

"Oh yes, quite serious," said the doctor gravely. "Why, there are three doctors there already!"

A YOUNG DOCTOR ASKED an older colleague, "Why do you always ask your patients what they've had for dinner?"

"It's very simple. I make out the bill according to the dinner menu!"

AN AGING BUT STILL HAUGHTY DOCTOR called one of his assistants into the office. "You know, I've had a marvelous and unique life," he said, "but I'm getting along in years and I think it's time I thought about my death. I'd like you to go out and find a nice resting place for me."

A few days later the assistant returned with pictures of a cemetery site on the side of a hill that got a lot of sun and had a stream nearby.

WHAT'S UP, DOC?

"This looks wonderful!" beamed the doctor. "How much is it?"

"Well, sir, this lot is four hundred thousand dollars."

"Four hundred thousand dollars! But I'm only going to be there four days!"

A RENOWNED DOCTOR was addressing a class of graduating medical students.

"Soon you will go out into the world," he said, "and you will have to weigh the cost of your education against the size of your fees. For myself I felt it was best to specialize. Now, I get five hundred dollars an hour for house calls, two hundred dollars an hour for office visits, and one hundred dollars for advice over the phone."

"Hey Doctor," called out one of the students, "how much do you get if you pass one of your patients on the street?"

Two psychiatrists bumped into each other in the hospital cafeteria. "How am I feeling?" asked the first one of the second.

"Oh, just fine," said the second doctor. "How am I feeling?"

A gray-haired woman went to the doctor complaining of swollen ankles. The doctor gave her anti-swelling pills and instructed her to take one every other day.

"I'm sorry, doctor," said the lady, "I'm not sure I understand the treatment."

"It's very simple," said the doctor. "Take one pill today, skip tomorrow, take one pill the next day, skip the day after that, and continue that way until the prescription is finished. Come back and see me then."

A few weeks later the woman returned, and her ankles looked completely normal. The doctor was pleased. "It looks like it worked. I think you can stop the treatment."

"Oh, good," said the old woman. "I didn't mind the pills, but the skipping was killing me!"

WHAT'S UP, DOC?

"MY STOMACH HAS BEEN BOTHERING ME, Doctor," complained the patient.

"What have you been eating?" asked the doctor.

"That's easy. I only eat pool balls."

"Pool balls?!" said the astonished doctor. "Maybe that's the trouble. What kind do you eat?"

"All kinds," replied the man. "Red ones for breakfast, yellow and orange for lunch, blue in the afternoon, and purple and black for dinner."

"I see the problem," said the doctor. "You haven't been getting any greens!"

THE DOCTOR APPEARED at his patient's bed with something strange behind his ear. As the patient looked closer, he said to the doctor, "Hey, Doc, you've got a suppository behind your ear!"

"What?!" exclaimed the doctor. "That means some asshole has my pencil!"

A MAN WENT TO HIS DOCTOR with an embarrassing problem. "Doc, you won't believe this, but my penis has holes in it!"

"That's silly," said the doctor. "Everybody's penis has a hole in it."

"No, Doc, you don't understand, I know about everyone's penis. I mean that mine has a lot of holes in it. When I go to the bathroom, it goes all over my pants. And at work, I soak the guy next to me!"

The doctor thought for a few minutes, and finally passed the man a name and address.

"What is this?" asked the man, "The name of a specialist?"

"Sort of," said the doctor. "It's the address of my brother. He plays trumpet in a jazz band. I'll have him give you a few lessons!"

THE YOUNG DOCTOR came in to deliver the bad news. "I'm sorry, Mr. Jones, but you only have three minutes to live."

WHAT'S UP, DOC?

"Oh, that's terrible. Is there anything you can do?"

"Hmmm, let me think," said the doctor, rubbing his chin. "You know, if I start right now, I might be able to boil an egg!"

A DOCTOR AND A LAWYER were talking at a party. "You know," said the doctor, "I hate when people come up to me and tell me what's wrong with them. Then they expect me to dish out free advice right on the spot. Does that ever happen to you?"

"Oh sure," said the lawyer.

"What do you do?"

"Well, the next morning I send them a bill that says 'Fees incurred at party last night—twenty-five dollars'. That soon stops it."

"That's a good idea. I'll try it!"

The next morning the doctor got a letter from the lawyer that said, "Fees incurred at party last night—twenty-five dollars."

Suds Lanigan

A MAN WITH A TERRIBLE STUTTER went to a specialist to look for a cure. After a thorough examination, the doctor told him to have three inches taken off his penis in order to cure the stutter. The man reluctantly agreed, the operation took place, and the man left without a trace of the stuttering.

But a few weeks later, he returned to the office to confront the doctor, "Doctor, it's great not to stutter, but my wife is very upset with my new situation. Is there any way to reverse the operation?"

The doctor looked at him. "I d-d-d-d-don't th-th-th-think s-s-s-s-so."

"DOCTOR! DOCTOR! You have to see my wife right away! I think she has appendicitis!"

"That's impossible! Your wife had her appendix out last year. Have you ever seen anybody with a second appendix?"

"Have you ever seen anybody with a second wife?"

WHAT'S UP, DOC?

✚

"Hello, Mrs. Johnson. This is Dr. Olean calling. I'm here with the results of your pregnancy test and I have some terrific news."

"My name is Miss Johnson and my boyfriend just ran off with a nurse!"

"Oh . . . in that case I'm here with the results of your pregnancy test and I have some bad news!"

✚

Mrs. Rush burst into the doctor's office. "Doctor! Am I mad at you! My husband came to you two months ago with headaches. Since he saw you, he stays out late, never comes home on the weekend, and hardly even looks at me anymore!"

The Doctor was shocked. "I can't believe it! All I did was give him a new set of glasses!"

✚

A BEAUTIFUL DARK-HAIRED YOUNG GIRL arrived at the gates of heaven.

"Are you a virgin?" asked St. Peter.

"Of course," said the girl.

"In this day and age we can never be too sure. I have scheduled an appointment for you with the Heavenly Physician."

A few hours later, St. Peter got the report and looked over at the young woman.

"It seems you have seven small dents in your hymen, but it isn't broken. So, I suppose we can't keep you out of heaven for that. What is your name?"

"Snow White."

A NERVOUS WOMAN went to the dentist.

"You know, doctor, I hate having work done on my teeth. In fact, I think I would rather give birth than have a tooth drilled."

"Great," said the dentist. "But you'd better make up your mind before I adjust the chair!"

WHAT'S UP, DOC?

A MAN WAS HAVING severe stomach pains and called the doctor for an appointment. The busy physician told him that he had no openings for a week. In desperation, the man went to his pharmacist and begged for something to ease the pain. The following week, he arrived at the doctor's office at the appointed time.

"You know, doctor," said the man, "the pharmacist gave me this blue concoction, and told me to take it every three hours. He also told me to avoid physical activity and red meat, but none of it did any good."

The doctor said rather coldly, "I know that man and he has a reputation for giving lousy advice. What else did he say?"

"He told me to come see you!"

A MAN WENT TO THE DOCTOR and heard the news that he had an inoperable brain tumor. Even worse, the doctor told him that he had only twenty-four hours to live.

He went home very upset to tell his wife the dreadful news. "What can I do to make your last day easier?" asked his wife.

"Make love to me," said the man.

They went to bed, and afterward, his wife asked what else she might do. "Make love to me again," said the man.

They went on like this for nearly twenty hours, and every time they finished, the husband asked to make love again.

Wearily, the wife asked, "What can I do to make your last four hours easier?"

Turning to her, he said, "Make love to me again."

"Hey, I have to get up in the morning!"

Mr. Michaels went to the dentist to have a tooth removed. However, every time the dentist began to pull it out the patient would clamp his mouth shut. Trying to find a solution, the dentist pulled his assistant aside.

"The next time I reach for the tooth, I want you to take these forceps and give Mr. Michaels a big pinch in the side."

On his next attempt, the nurse administered a vicious pinch and Mr. Michaels' mouth flew open. The tooth was extracted.

"Well, Mr. Michaels, that didn't hurt much, did it?" asked the doctor.

"Not too bad," commented Mr. Michaels.

"But who would have thought the roots went so deep?"

✚

A YOUNG MAN WENT TO A PARTY and met a very attractive young blonde. She seemed very agreeable and after a few drinks she invited him to her apartment around the corner. Soon they were naked, and she told him that she had been to the doctor that day and diagnosed to have a disease, but she couldn't remember what.

"Do you have any idea?" asked the man.

"It started with an 'a.' It was either AIDS or arthritis, I can't remember which."

Quickly, the man called a doctor friend of his, but the friend couldn't do the diagnosis over the phone.

"But I have an idea," said the doctor. "Chase her around the room a little, and if her joints swell, then make love to her!"

✚

A NERVOUS NEW FATHER rushed into the hospital maternity ward where his wife had given birth. The doctor greeted him. "Mr. Jones, I think I should take you down to the nursery. I have something to show you."

"Doc, I'm so nervous," blurted out the man.

"Don't worry, that's perfectly natural," said the doctor.

Holding his hands over his eyes, the man said, "I don't think I can look!"

"I really think you ought to see this," said the doctor.

"Will you tell me what you see?" asked the man.

"Of course," assured the doctor.

"Is it a boy?"

The doctor scratched his forehead. "The one in the middle is!"

"DOCTOR! DOCTOR! I can't sleep at night!"
"Sleep during the day!"

WHAT'S UP, DOC?

An elderly couple went to the doctor. "What can I do for you?" the doctor asked.

"Doctor, we have a strange request. We'd like you to watch us make love."

Puzzled but willing, the doctor watched as the couple took off their clothes and began to have sex in his office. When they were through, they dressed and the doctor presented them with a bill for ten dollars. "From what I observed there is nothing wrong with the way in which you engage in sexual intercourse. In fact, I hope to have that much stamina at your age!" he said.

"Thanks, Doctor," they both said as they left. They returned a week later and everything was repeated. This continued for a couple of weeks, at ten dollars a visit, until finally the doctor asked, "Look, I made it clear that there was nothing wrong with your technique. Why do you keep coming back?"

The man shyly answered, "It's like this. She's married so we can't go at her house. I'm married, so we can't meet at mine. The No-Tell Motel charges twenty-seven dollars for two hours. You only charge ten dollars, and I get eight dollars back in Medicare!"

Suds Lanigan

A MAN WALKED INTO a psychiatrist's office with a large box. The psychiatrist sat the man down. "For this to be a successful relationship, you will have to trust me. Now, what is in the box?"

The man opened the box to reveal a woman's severed head, wearing a large flowered hat.

"Oh my God," gasped the psychiatrist. "That's awful!"

"See, Doctor, that's exactly what I told her when she bought it!"

A RICH OLD WOMAN, married and divorced many times, found yet another man willing to marry her, despite her advancing years and past record. Just before the wedding, she went to see her plastic surgeon, a trip she had made often. When she told the doctor that she wanted another face-lift, he objected.

"You've had about twenty face-lifts already, it would be both difficult and dangerous for you to have another."

"Oh please, you must," the woman said. "I'm going to get married again, and to a much younger man. I can't walk down the

WHAT'S UP, DOC?

aisle looking like this! Please!" But the doctor was unmoved.

"All right," the woman said. "I'll throw in an extra ten thousand if you do it. I'm desperate." The doctor was suddenly moved with pity and decided to perform the operation.

After the operation, the woman admired her face in the mirror. "Doctor, it looks marvelous! And it wasn't dangerous at all. One thing though," she said, fingering her chin, "I don't remember having a dimple. And it's so large!"

The doctor stroked his chin. "I'm afraid it isn't a dimple at all. It's your navel. If I lift your face anymore you'll be shaving!"

✚

JOSHUA AND HIS BABY BROTHER were playing together in their room, when for no apparent reason, his little brother bit Joshua.

"Mom, I can't believe it, I wasn't doing anything to him, I swear. The baby just up and bit my finger. What are you going to do to him about it?" Joshua demanded of his mother.

His mother smiled at him. "Joshua, don't worry about it. He's teething."

"But it hurt!" Joshua wailed.

"Joshua, you can't blame him, he's teething," his mother said. "He doesn't even know it hurts when he bites you."

A few minutes later, she heard the baby crying. "Joshua, what's going on." she asked.

"It's all right Mom," Joshua said, "he knows now."

✠

A RICH MAN WENT TO THE HOSPITAL because of sharp pains he was experiencing in his legs. After a few days there for tests, his doctor came back. "Mr. Strong, I have some good news and some bad news for you. Which one do you want first?"

The man looked down at the ground and asked for the bad news first. "All right, the bad news is that I think I'm gonna have to amputate both your legs."

"My legs!" cried the man. "What on earth could the good news be?"

"The man in the next room says he'll buy your slippers."

WHAT'S UP, DOC?

A MAN WENT TO SEE his doctor for a routine check-up.

"Doctor, could you please hurry? I've got an appointment at twelve o'clock."

"No problem," the doctor said. "In fact, I have a new computer that can give you a complete diagnosis just from a urine sample."

The doctor gave the man a specimen cup and directed him to the bathroom. The man returned with the cup filled. The doctor then took the filled cup and poured its contents into a hole in the machine. The machine clicked and whirred for a few moments, then spat out a piece of paper.

"Hmmm," the doctor said while he looked over the paper. "It says here that you suffer from tennis elbow."

"What?" the man exclaimed. "I don't even play tennis, and my elbow feels fine. That computer doesn't know what it's talking about."

"Please sir, the computer has never been wrong yet. Are you sure you're experiencing no pain in your elbow?" the doctor asked.

"Positive."

"Okay, no need to get upset. I'll make you a deal. You come back here tomorrow morning with a sample and we'll test you again for no charge."

"All right. But you better have that thing fixed before I get here."

The man was given a new cup and then he left. On the way home he got madder and madder over the idea of a lousy machine that was the final judge of his health. "These stinkin' machines," he muttered. "I know just the way to screw it up."

When he got home, the man urinated into the cup until it was half-filled. Then he went out to the car and took the dipstick out of his engine and swished it around until the liquid turned black. Then, he persuaded his wife and daughter to donate some urine into the mix. Finally, before he went off to bed, he masturbated into the cup. The next day, barely concealing his glee, he went into the doctor's office where the doctor greeted him.

"Hello, glad to see you," said the doctor. "Do you have the urine?"

"Yes, right here," the man said, and handed him the cup.

The doctor looked suspiciously at the murky fluid, but then just shrugged and poured it into the machine. Again, the machine clicked and whirred for a few moments, and spat out another piece of paper. The doctor perused the diagnosis.

"Well sir, it seems that your car is a quart low, your wife is pregnant, your daughter has gonorrhea and your tennis elbow is only going to get worse if you keep whacking off like that!"

A YOUNG MAN looking very disturbed walked into the doctor's office.

"Doctor, I have a very serious problem. I can't, you know, go to the bathroom."

"What do you mean, son?" asked the doctor.

"I can't do number two, you know, drop a load, excremate, defecate, crap . . ."

"I see. Well here," the doctor said. "This prescription will have you running like a faucet."

A few weeks later, the young man returned. "Doc, I still can't do it. I'm in the bathroom for hours and not a drop."

"Hmm, that's strange. Here, this prescription is a little stronger. It ought to do the trick."

"I sure hope so," the young man said.

A few weeks later, the man returned, discomfort written all over his face. "Still nothing, Doc. It's been months."

"I don't believe it," said the doctor. "The stuff I gave you could clear up constipation in an elephant. By the way, what do you do for a living?"

"I'm an unpublished writer."

"Well, why didn't you tell me before?" the doctor said as he reached into his pocket for some money. "Here, go out and get yourself some food."

AFTER MANY YEARS OF MARRIAGE a doctor became restless, and began to have an affair with a nurse. Within weeks, the nurse became pregnant. They were both in a quandary about what to do with a child, as neither one of them wanted to become a parent. Their indecision lasted nine months, at which point the nurse went into labor and was rushed to the hospital. About the same time, a priest was admitted for surgery on his prostate gland. This gave the doctor an idea.

"I think I know what we can do with the baby," he told the nurse right before she entered the delivery room. "There's a priest here and I'm performing the operation. We can give him the child! We'll tell him that he miraculously gave birth to it during the operation."

The nurse was dubious, but desperate, so she reluctantly agreed. Soon after the birth, the doctor completed the priest's surgery.

"Father, I have something to tell you," the doctor whispered to the recovering priest. "Something that you will find absolutely extraordinary."

"What is it? Did the operation go all right?" the priest asked groggily.

"The operation was fine, but while I was performing surgery, you gave birth to this child." With that the doctor presented him with the baby.

"What! Why, this is impossible. How could this possibly have happened?" the astounded priest managed to gasp out.

"It's a miracle," the doctor said, and looked up at the ceiling. "Thank the Lord."

The priest took the baby home. Years went by, and the child grew into adolescence. One day, the priest decided to tell the child the truth and called the boy into his study.

"Son, I have something to tell you," the priest began.

"What is it?" asked the boy.

"Well son, I'm not really your father."

"What? What are you saying?" cried the boy.

The priest continued. "I'm your mother. The archbishop is your father."

✠

A PATIENT WALKED INTO the doctor's office to find out the results of some tests he had taken.

The doctor rushed him into his office and began quickly. "I've got some bad news, and some really bad news."

"What is it?" the patient asked.

The doctor went on. "The bad news is that the tests show you only have twenty-four hours to live."

"Oh my God! That's terrible. But what could possibly be worse than that?"

"I've been trying to reach you since yesterday."

✠

WHAT'S UP, DOC?

A YOUNG MAN WENT TO THE HOSPITAL to have some surgery performed to relieve him of his hemorrhoidal problems. After the operation, the surgeon walked into the post-operation ward with a grim look on his face.

"Son, I've got some bad news. Somehow, while we were operating, you got turned around so that we ended up cutting off your penis instead of treating your hemorrhoids."

"What!?" the young man exclaimed. "Does this mean I'll never again experience an erection?"

"Well, you might," corrected the doctor, "but it just won't be yours."

✚

BOB HAD BEEN EMBARRASSED all of his life about the size of his penis. It was so small that women laughed at him and men in the locker room pointed and stared. Finally he decided to do something. He went to the doctor and explained the problem.

The doctor wasn't terribly reassuring. "Unfortunately, there is nothing that we can do. It's something you are just going to have to live with. However . . . there is some experimental surgery . . . but I couldn't . . ."

"Oh please, Doc, I'm desperate. I'll try anything!"

"No, I'm sorry, it's just too dangerous. It's still in the experimental stage. It hasn't been successfully performed on an animal yet."

After much argument, the doctor decided to give it a try. The operation involved having a section of an elephant trunk sewn on the end of Bob's penis. The operation was a rousing success, and Bob's outlook changed completely. For the first time in years, he was going on a date.

When they arrived at the restaurant, Bob was talking on when he noticed the woman staring at the bulge in his trousers. They had been seated a few minutes when an elephant trunk reached out, dipped in the bread basket, and disappeared. The woman was amazed.

"Bob, can you do that again?" she asked.

"I could," said Bob, squirming. "But I'm not sure my asshole could take another bread stick!"

THE NURSE WENT INTO THE HOSPITAL room to see about the condition of the aged Mr.

WHAT'S UP, DOC?

Greene, who was receiving all his sustenance by way of an enema.

"I have a treat for you today, Mr. Greene," she announced as she pushed the tray up to the bed.

"What could it possibly be, nurse?" groused Mr. Greene. "I get all my meals through an enema."

"That's true. But today we're giving you hot chocolate." Mr. Greene brightened visibly and turned on his side to receive the treat. But almost immediately he began to writhe in discomfort.

"What's the matter?" asked the concerned nurse. "Too hot?"

"Noooooo," grimaced Mr. Greene. "Too sweet."

MRS. ROGOVIN WAS TALKING to one of her friends on the telephone. Her favorite subject for discussion was herself, with her son a close second. Mrs. Rogovin blathered on.

"You know my son, well you'd never guess what he's doing. He's going to a psychiatrist three times a week. I'm so pleased."

Her friend on the other end said, "You're

pleased that your son is going to a psychiatrist?"

"Sure," Mrs. Rogovin said. "And he's spending an incredible amount of money to do it."

Her friend was still just as confused. "Why on earth does that make you happy?"

"Well," Mrs. Rogovin said grandly, "from what he tells me, he spends all that time just talking about me!"

AN ELDERLY DOCTOR, well along in years, decided it was time to turn over his medical practice to his young son fresh out of internship. The son, though well-versed in the latest techniques at big-city hospitals, was unfamiliar with the small-town practice of his father. So the old doctor decided to show him the ropes as he took his son around on his calls.

"One thing you always have to remember as a small-town doctor is that many times people won't tell you all you need to know to make a diagnosis," the old doctor lectured as they were driving. "Sometimes it's because they're ashamed or they're shy or they just

WHAT'S UP, DOC?

don't like you. Nevertheless, we have to help them. So the first rule is that you must always be observant. Noticing things that perhaps they are unwilling to tell you can simplify matters. For instance, Mrs. Johnson is overweight. But her problem isn't glandular as she contends. Her problem is that she stuffs herself with pork rinds. I saw dozens of empty wrappers in her garbage when we were there this morning.

"And Mr. Wade, he complains about having no energy. That's because he drinks his dinner. I had to climb over mountains of scotch bottles to get into his house. So remember, save yourself time and be observant."

At the next stop the older doctor knocked. When there was no response, the two men went on up the stairs to investigate. To their surprise, there was a beautiful woman in bed. A bit flustered, she told them about her problem—she was having anxiety attacks. The older doctor stepped back to let his son handle the case. The young doctor bent over the patient, listened to her increased heartbeat, and saw the beads of sweat on her forehead. He decided to check her temperature, but he fumbled the thermometer and it fell on the floor next to her bed. He bent over and picked it up, and went on with his examination.

When he had finished the examination, he made his diagnosis. "I think you're working too hard on the political side of your life. If you stop concentrating so much on that, I guarantee your attacks will subside." The woman sat up in her bed and nervously thanked him.

When the doctors got back to their car, the older one asked him, "How on earth could you give her such specific advice?"

"Just followed your rule of simple deduction and observation," the young doctor answered. "When I bent over to pick up the thermometer, I noticed the mayor under the bed."

✚

TWO DOCTORS, part of a medical rescue team, were patrolling the western coast of Ireland in the wake of one of the most dreadful storms in memory. The medical team was searching for survivors and victims of the hurricane in need of medical attention.

While there was much wreckage from ships and broken docks and the occasional house washed from the shore, the search had not yet turned up any bodies. Eventually, however, they spotted something that looked like a figure along the beach. When they got closer they could see it was the nude body of a lifeless woman who had apparently been washed up on the shore. And on top of the woman was a man humping away. The two doctors approached the man. One of them tapped him on the shoulder.

"Excuse me, sir, do you know that's a dead woman?"

The man looked up, an astonished expression on his face. "Oh, my God! I thought she was Irish."

✠

A WELL-KNOWN BOSTON CARDIOLOGIST in his late sixties was being interviewed by a reporter from a medical journal.

"Tell me, doctor. You've had a long and distinguished medical career. Have you ever made a mistake?"

"Just one," the doctor sighed. "I once cured a millionaire in only three visits."

✠

IN THE MIDDLE OF THE NIGHT, three psychological test rats begin to talk.

"I'm very confused. I don't think I understand my supervisor," said the first.

"I think my supervisor is kind of slow," said the second.

"I've got mine trained perfectly," said the third. "Every time I run through the maze, he has to feed me!"

A MAN GOES TO THE DOCTOR and the doctor says, "It's very serious. I must operate immediately."

"But Doc, I feel fine. This was just supposed to be a check-up!"

"I know, I know, these things are difficult to take. It's also going to be expensive. It will cost five thousand dollars."

"But Doc, I don't have that kind of money!"

"I know, I know, but I will make it easy on you. I will operate now, and you can pay me back a little each month."

"Oh, kind of like you're buying a car!"

"Well, I am."

WHAT'S UP, DOC?

THE TELEPHONE RANG in the middle of the night. Mr. Jensen, the plumber, picked it up and groggily said hello.

"Jensen, this is Dr. Ward. I need your help."

"Dr. Ward," the plumber replied, "it must be two in the morning. What on earth are you calling me now for?"

"My bathroom pipes are all stopped up," the doctor replied, and he went on to explain the situation at great length. Finally he was interrupted by the plumber who said wearily, "Tell you what you do, Doctor. Drop two aspirin down the toilet and call me in the morning."

A VERY SEXY-LOOKING BLONDE sauntered into the doctor's waiting room. The office was full of patients and she looked around in vain for an empty seat. Finally she walked over to one man and said in a low husky voice, "I wonder if I might trouble you for a seat. You see, I'm pregnant."

The man quickly stood up and offered his chair to the young woman. As she sat down he looked her over admiringly. "I must say you certainly don't look pregnant. How far along are you?"

She looked up and smiled. "Oh, it's only been half an hour."

The man walked into the office of the eminent psychiatrist Dr. Von Bernuth, and sat down to explain his problem.

"Doctor, Doctor," he started.

"No need to repeat yourself, my good man," replied the doctor. "One 'Doctor' is enough."

"Yes, well, you see, I've got this problem," the man continued. "I keep hallucinating that I'm a dog. A large white hairy Pyrenees mountain dog. It's crazy. I don't know what to do."

"A common canine complex," said the doctor soothingly. "Come over here and lie down on the couch."

"Oh no, Doctor. I'm not allowed up on the furniture."

WHAT'S UP, DOC?

THE TWO FATHERS were peering at their new babies through the glass in the maternity ward. The younger of the two men proudly announced that the little baby girl was his first child, to which the other replied that the little baby boy was his fifth child.

"Fifth!" the first man exclaimed. "Wow! Well, since you've been here before, let me ask you a very personal question. How long after the baby's born can my wife and I make love?"

The second man looked over. "That all depends on whether you have a private or semi-private room."

A MAN WALKED INTO THE DOCTOR'S OFFICE to find out the results of a series of tests that he had undergone. His worst fears were confirmed.

"I'm afraid I have some bad news for you, Mr. McIntosh. You're going to die in four weeks."

The man was distraught. "Doctor, that's terrible! I want a second opinion."

"Well, you're ugly too."

AN EXTREMELY OBESE MAN went to the doctor to see what could be done about his problem of overeating. "Look, Doctor, I've tried all kinds of bizarre diets and appetite suppressants, and not one of them has worked. I'm still two hundred pounds overweight."

The doctor looked over at the man and, even without examining, nodded his head in agreement.

"I've recently heard of a new weight-loss method," said the doctor, "but its still in the experimental stage. It's called the Per Rectum diet. What that means is that you can no longer eat anything through your mouth, but must inhale it, as it were, through the rectum. Here's the article in the medical journal. Try the diet and come back at the first of the month."

A few weeks later the man returned, looking quite a bit slimmer. "Mr. Snyder, I'm impressed," admired the doctor. "You've lost twenty-five pounds. Tell me, have there been any negative side-effects?"

The man thought before replying. "Well, it itches a little, but otherwise it's been fine."

The doctor was pleased. "Okay, keep going on the diet and I'll see you in a few weeks."

As the man made his way out of the office, the doctor noticed that he was walking with a strange gait. "Excuse me," the doctor said, "you said there were no side-effects. Why are you walking that way?"

"No problem, doctor. I'm just chewing some gum."

AN INTERN HAD A ROOMMATE with a horrible smoking problem. Every night, the roommate would have continuous coughing fits, and in the morning would look terrible. The intern lectured him again and again. "I told you cigarettes are unhealthy. If you don't take care of yourself, one night you're going to cough your guts out."

The next month the doctor became engaged to be married, and he and his roommate went for one last night of bachelor fun. They staggered back home, the intern's friend much the worse of the two. The roommate collapsed onto his bed and fell into a deep sleep. Then the intern, as a joke, went to his lab at the hospital and picked up a sample of human intestines. He brought it home and dropped the intestines over his sleeping roommate's chest.

The next morning, the intern was up early drinking tea when the hungover roommate appeared in the doorway. The intern looked up and greeted his friend with a cheery, "Did you sleep well?"

The roommate, looked bewildered, could only grunt. "The strangest thing happened. I think I actually coughed up my guts."

The doctor suppressed a smile and said smugly, "Didn't I tell you to stop smoking? You could have avoided all this trouble."

His friend had a sick expression. "You don't know the half of it. After I noticed my intestines all over my chest, I had a heck of a time getting them back in."

WHAT'S UP, DOC?

A COLLEGE BASKETBALL STAR went to the team doctor about a problem he had with breaking wind.

"Doctor," the young man said, "I can't help myself. I'll be playing ball and whenever I go up for a shot, and fully extend my body, *boom!* a really loud fart comes out. I know it doesn't smell bad, but the sound of it throws off my teammates sometimes."

The doctor asked the young man to demonstrate. Moving a chair, the young man jumped as though he were going up for a shot. The doctor was treated to an ear-shattering display of the force of the young man's gas.

"I see your problem," said the doctor. "I can give you some pills to take care of the gas, but I'm afraid we're going to have to schedule an operation on your nose."

"My nose! There's nothing wrong with my nose. Why an operation?"

"Because, young man," replied the doctor, "that fart sure as hell stank!"

✚

A MAN, WORRIED about his rapid drop in weight, walked into his doctor's office. The doctor gave him a complete physical check-up and after examining the results sat his patient down.

"I'm afraid you have a tapeworm which has lodged in your intestines. It's an unusually large tapeworm and I'm not sure that regular medication will work in this case."

"But, Doctor," the patient protested, "there's gotta be something you can do about it."

"There is a rarely-used treatment that is very effective, and we could try it. Take off all of your clothes and lie down on your stomach, please." With that, the doctor went over to a cupboard and returned holding several objects.

Apprehensively, the man followed the instructions and was soon prone on the examination table. The doctor leaned over and deftly stuck an apple and two Oreo cookies into his ass.

"Excuse me, doctor, are you sure this is the right procedure?" the man winced.

"This is exactly the way it's done," the doctor replied with confidence. "Come back tomorrow at the same time."

The following day the man returned and the doctor repeated the procedure. And again the following day. On the fourth day the man reluctantly and painfully made his way into the doctor's office. Upon entering the exami-

WHAT'S UP, DOC?

nation room he noticed that the doctor was holding an apple, but in place of the two Oreos, he had a hammer.

"Lie down on your stomach, please," he said. The man reluctantly obeyed and once again felt the painful sensation of the apple inserted. The doctor, hammer in hand, waited a few moments, staring at the man's backside.

Finally, a tapeworm stuck its head out and asked, "Where are my two cookies?" And the doctor smacked it over the head.

A MILLIONAIRE, WELL ALONG IN YEARS, had a sharp pain in his chest. He turned to his young wife and gasped, "I'm having a heart attack. Quick. Buy me a hospital!"

A MAN WENT TO SEE HIS PSYCHIATRIST. "Doctor, you've got to help me. I find that I'm talking to myself all the time. Everywhere. In elevators, on the street, at parties. What can I do?"

The doctor leaned back. "Oh, I wouldn't worry about it. Lots of people talk to themselves all the time. It's perfectly normal."

The man shook his head. "Yeah, but you don't know what a bore I am!"

A POOR CARPENTER took his ailing wife to a doctor. The doctor examined her and ran some tests. Then he pulled the man aside. "Your wife is very sick and I'm afraid she might not have long to live. I can try and cure her, but it will be very expensive. What kind of insurance do you have?"

The distraught man looked at him. "Insurance? I don't have any insurance. But if you cure her I'll pay you anything. Anything!"

"But I could treat her and she still might die," said the doctor shrewdly.

"Just treat her," the man pleaded, "whether you cure her or kill her, I'll pay you whatever you ask, even if I have to sell everything."

The doctor agreed, but despite his treatment, the woman died within a week. Remembering the conversation, the doctor presented a huge bill to the grieving carpenter. "Ten thousand!" he gasped. "I can't pay this. Can we go to the judge in town and discuss some form of settlement?"

The doctor agreed and that afternoon the three men sat down to discuss the fee. First the judge heard from the carpenter. Then he turned to the doctor. Well aware of the doctor's reputation for large fees, the judge asked, "Did you cure this man's wife?"

"Alas, no," replied the doctor.

"Did you kill her?"

"Certainly not," protested the doctor.

"Well, under what terms of the agreement are you claiming a fee?"

A SICKLY MAN DRAGGED HIMSELF into the doctor's waiting room to get the results of the tests that had been performed on him. He slumped in a chair and then looked around at the only other patient waiting, a woman. And what a woman! A gorgeous brunette, in a short slinky dress which did nothing but accentuate her magnificent figure.

He had never seen such a spectacular-looking woman and he kept staring at her. Her looks almost took his mind off his fears about the test results. Soon the doctor came out.

"Mr. Johnson, the test results have come back and I've got some good news and bad news."

"What's the bad news?" the man gasped.

"The bad news is that all the tests show that you're going to die within a month."

"Oh, that's terrible," the man said. "Then what's the good news?"

"See that great-looking woman over there? I'm having an affair with her!"

✚

A MAN WALKED INTO A DOCTOR'S OFFICE. He was hunched over and walking with some amount of discomfort. When the doctor came out the man said, "Doctor, you've got to help me. I've got a twig sticking out of my ass."

The doctor showed him to the examination room and then instructed him to take down his pants.

"Doctor, I'm very modest. Is that really necessary?"

"My good man, replied the doctor impatiently, "I've got a number of sick people out there who need my help and you're telling me you have a twig sticking out. I can't make a diagnosis until I've examined you. Drop your drawers. Please!"

With that, the man undid his belt and dropped his trousers and bent over the examination table.

"I don't believe it," exclaimed the doctor. "You *do* have a twig sticking out!"

"It's very uncomfortable, Doctor. Please try and remove it."

The doctor put on rubber gloves, greased his hands and reached in to remove the twig. Slowly he pulled the twig out further and further. The twig was attached to a bouquet of roses.

"I don't believe it," marvelled the doctor. "Here's a dozen long-stem red roses. How'd they get there?"

"Never mind that," said the patient. "Read the card!"

✚

THE PATIENT WAS IN THE HOSPITAL recuperating after a quadruple bypass operation on his heart. The doctor had been visiting him every day for a week to see how the recovery was progressing. On this visit the patient was sitting up with his eyes open. Although still attached to numerous tubes and monitoring wires the patient looked much improved.

"How are we feeling today?" Dr. Goldberg asked.

"I'm feeling much better, thank you, Doctor, and I'm ready for you to give me your bill."

"Not yet," cautioned the doctor. "I don't think you're strong enough."

DR. CHARLTON WAS ATTENDING a dinner party and watching the host adroitly carve and slice the large turkey for his guests.

"How am I doing, Doctor? Pretty good, huh? I think I'd make a pretty good surgeon," said the host proudly.

When the host was through piling up the sliced turkey on the serving platter, the good physician observed, "Anyone can take them apart. Now let's see you put them back together again."

WHAT'S UP, DOC?

Eric was in the midst of a very competitive table tennis match when he accidentally caught a slammed ball in the mouth and swallowed it. Gasping for air, he was rushed to the emergency ward of the local hospital where surgery was performed.

When Eric awoke several hours later he looked up at the doctor and thanked him for saving his life. Then he looked down and saw about twelve sewn-up incisions on his stomach.

"Good gosh!" Eric exclaimed. "Why did you make so many cuts?"

The doctor spread his palms. "That's the way the ball bounces."

A retired baseball player, in poor health and down on his luck, was in need of an operation. He asked around and was finally directed to the most respected and expensive specialist in town.

"Doc, I've been told that I need this expensive operation," he explained.

"I'm afraid it'll cost you ten thousand dollars. In advance," replied the doctor.

"What! Hey, Doctor, c'mon, times are tough, I didn't make the big bucks. I can't afford that," replied the old ballplayer.

"Okay, I'll tell you what I'll do, the doctor responded. "I used to be a big fan of yours. I'll call it a thousand and you send me one of your old uniforms."

"That's still too steep," replied the old pro.

They haggled back and forth, and finally settled on fifty dollars and the baseball cap the old-timer had worn in the World Series.

"At that price, I might as well do it for free!" said the doctor, shaking his head. "Tell me, if you knew I was the most expensive doctor in town, and you knew you couldn't afford it, why did you come here?"

"Hey, Doc, where my health is concerned, money is no object."

Mr. Norton was in the hospital recovering from an operation. The nurse on duty received a call from a man who asked, "How is Mr. Norton doing?"

"Oh, quite well. We expect he'll be released in the morning."

"Very good, thank you."

"May I ask who is calling so that I can tell Mr. Norton?" inquired the nurse.

"This is Mr. Norton. The doctors don't tell me a damn thing!"

A MAN WALKED INTO HIS DOCTOR'S OFFICE to hear the results of some tests he had taken the previous week.

Ushered into the doctor's office the man asked anxiously, "Okay, Dr. Mirsky, give it to me straight."

Shaking his head, the doctor replied, "Well, to be honest with you, Mr. Dunne, you only have six months to live."

"Oh my God!," said the man slumping down in his chair. "Is there anything I can do?"

"One thing. Marry a fat woman, have three hyperactive children, and move to Detroit."

The patient was confused. "Will that help me live longer?"

"No," replied the doctor, "but it will sure seem like it."

✚

AFTER SIX MONTHS OF THERAPY with a patient, the psychiatrist could stand it no longer. "The smoking!" blurted out the therapist. "You've got to give up smoking!"

"Smoking?" replied the man, "Smoking is the key to my disorder?"

"No, of course not," said the doctor. "But at least you'll stop burning holes in my couch!"

✚

A DISTINGUISHED-LOOKING OLDER MAN walked into a psychiatrist's office. When the psychiatrist began talking to him and filling out the preliminary forms, the man took out a pouch of tobacco, and began stuffing its contents into his ears.

The doctor looked up at him and said, "Well, sir, I think you have come to the right place for treatment. Is there anything I can do for you first?"

"Yeah," said the man. "Do you have a light?"

"DOCTOR! DOCTOR!" CRIED OUT THE MAN as he rushed into the doctor's office. "I think I have amnesia!"

The doctor was concerned. "When did you first notice it?"

"Notice what?"

A BLUE-HAIRED OLDER WOMAN waddled into the doctor's office and said, "Doctor, I don't feel so good."

The doctor was very familiar with the woman. "Mrs. Krapinski, some things even modern medicine can't cure. I can't make you any younger, you know."

"What? Who asked you to make me any

younger?" she answered, mopping her brow. "All I want is for you to make me older!"

On his first visit to the psychiatrist, Mr. Bakalar was given the Rorschach ink blot analysis. The doctor showed him the first picture and asked him what it looked like.

"That is two dogs having sex," replied Mr. Bakalar.

After the second ink blot, the man answered, "That is a nude woman in the shower."

On the third one, the man said, "That is a pair of crotchless underwear."

The entire test continued in this manner, and when it was complete, the doctor put the cards in a pile and looked at the patient. "Well, Mr. Bakalar, you do seem very preoccupied with sex."

"Me?!" Mr. Bakalar replied. "You're the pervert who keeps showing me all the dirty pictures!"

WHAT'S UP, DOC?

THE OLD LION, KING OF THE JUNGLE, went to see the jungle doctor about his problem with insomnia. A flock of birds had settled in his mane and were arguing so late into the night that he couldn't sleep. The jungle doctor told the lion to go home and put a pound of yeast in his pajamas and the birds would go away.

The old lion didn't believe it, but he did as he was told. Much to his surprise, the cure worked and the birds left the next night. He went to thank the jungle doctor, and offer some payment for the successful treatment.

"Oh, you don't need to worry about that!" answered the doctor, waving away the payment. "You are the King of the Jungle!"

"But surely you must need something to support yourself after your years of schooling?" growled the lion.

"Years of schooling? This is all common sense," said the doctor. "Surely you know that yeast is yeast and nest is nest, and never the mane shall tweet!"

A VERY SEXY YOUNG WOMAN, clad in a short skirt and revealing blouse, reported to the city hospital for her scheduled operation. After the operation, the doctor was at her bedside and asked how she was feeling.

"Very well, thank you, Dr. Karraker, but I was wondering if the scar will show."

"My dear," replied the doctor, "that is entirely up to you."

A WOMAN BRUSHED PAST THE NURSE and grabbed the doctor's sleeve.

"Doctor! Doctor!" she cried. "My husband is a sex maniac! He wants to do it all the time. Before breakfast, after breakfast, on the way to work, during lunch, before dinner, after dinner, and then over and over again all night long. Why, the other day he came up to me at the freezer and we were doing it again!"

The doctor looked at her. "The freezer doesn't sound any stranger than the other places you mentioned."

"At the supermarket?"

WHAT'S UP, DOC?

✚

An exhausted-looking man dragged himself into the doctor's office.

"Doctor, there are dogs all over my neighborhood. They bark all day and all night, and I can never get a wink of sleep!"

"I have good news for you," the doctor answered, rummaging through a drawer full of sample medications. "Here are some new sleeping pills that work like a dream. A few of these and your trouble will be over."

"Anything, Doctor. I'll give it a shot."

A few weeks later the man returned, looking worse than ever.

"Doc, your plan is no good. I'm more tired than before!"

"I don't understand how that could be," said the doctor shaking his head. "Those are the strongest pills on the market!"

"That may be true," the man answered wearily, "but I'm up all night chasing these dogs, and when I finally catch one it's hell getting him to swallow the pill!"

✚

A FAMOUS HEART SURGEON DIED and went to Heaven. When he arrived he found himself at the end of a mile-long line at the Pearly Gates. Not used to waiting for anything, the impatient doctor marched straight to the gate and confronted St. Peter.

"Listen. Do you know who I am? I am Dr. Harris, the famous heart surgeon! I have saved hundreds of lives!"

"Sorry, friend," answered St. Peter. "We get famous people here every day. Please go to the end of the line with everybody else."

Annoyed, Dr. Harris reluctantly retreated to the end of the queue. While shuffling his feet and growing impatient, he noticed a young intern go straight past the line right through the Pearly Gates into Heaven. Annoyed, Dr. Harris made his way back up to the head of the line and yelled at St. Peter.

"How could you possibly let that scrawny little doctor into heaven before a man of my stature?"

"That was no intern," corrected St. Peter. "That was God. He just likes to play doctor."

WHAT'S UP, DOC?

A YOUNG DOCTOR went to look at a practice that was for sale in a remote part of West Virginia. The situation seemed perfect: comfortable house, adequately equipped lab, lovely flower, vegetable and herb garden, fruit trees and a large barn with chickens and several cows. The old doctor who was showing the place quoted a very affordable price.

"This looks great," said the young doctor. "But how could you get such a nice set-up in an area with no real wealth, and the patients so far apart?"

"Well, I'll tell you," said the doctor. "It's just simple backwoods common sense and a strong work ethic. For example, most people around here take a vacation in the summer and spend a few weeks in the city or visiting relatives. But the wife and I spend the time at home, gardening and putting things in order. We cut our own firewood for heat, grow our own fruit and vegetables and have plenty from the livestock. The herb garden gives us a big harvest, and we mix the herbs and boil them into my secret tonic."

"Well, that seems great," admired the young man, "but that doesn't really explain this fine house and all of this land."

The doctor continued. "In the summer when the people come back from vacation, I tell them, 'You know, Mrs. Ruggles, you don't look too good. Is anything wrong?' And they usually say something like 'Well, vacation took a lot out of me.' "

" 'I know what you mean,' I tell them. 'Why don't you come by my office and I'll give you some of my good old-fashioned tonic?' At three dollars a bottle it really adds up."

"Yes, but making the tonic seems like an expensive process."

"No. A few weeks after the patient buys the tonic, I tell them, 'You know, Mrs. Ruggles, you are looking much better.' That way they feel like the medicine is working. Then I have them come in for a check-up, just to make sure everything is all right, and I tell them to bring a specimen. That way, you see, I get all my bottles back."

✠

A MAN WALKED into the doctor's office with a banana in his ear.

The doctor came out and said, "You know, son, you have a banana in your ear."

"Sorry, Doc, I can't hear you. I have a banana in my ear."

WHAT'S UP, DOC?

A YOUNG MAN GOT MARRIED to a famous and beautiful model. In a rush to impress his new bride, the groom had made many improvements to their house. In his haste, however, he forgot to tell his wife that he had lacquered the toilet seat, and when she used the bathroom she became glued to the seat. The distraught groom was forced to unbolt the toilet seat, wrap his bride in a raincoat and race to the emergency room of the local hospital. Speeding past a full waiting room, the man rushed her into the office of the doctor on duty where the young bride reluctantly bared all for the doctor.

"Well, what do you think?" asked the anxious groom.

"Very nice," clucked the doctor. "Really quite impressive. But why did you have it framed?"

Suds Lanigan

The new father was sitting in the waiting room of the maternity ward, disconsolate and dejected because his wife had given birth to a baby girl rather than the boy that he had been hoping for.

A nurse on duty came over to the man to comfort him. "Don't worry," said the nurse, "in a couple of months you'll forget you ever wanted a boy."

"Oh, it's okay, nurse," replied the man. "If I couldn't have a boy, this was my second choice."

✚

A man walked into a doctor's office and started pacing up and down the room.

"What seems to be your problem?" asked the doctor patiently.

"I don't know what it is, doctor," said the man gesturing wildly. "I go around thinking I'm a teepee. I mean a wigwam. I mean a teepee. NO, I mean a wigwam."

"Sit down," said the doctor. "You're too tents."

WHAT'S UP, DOC?

The maternity ward waiting room was full of nervous fathers-to-be pacing up and down. One nervous man blurted out to another standing across from him, "I'm so annoyed! This had to happen on our vacation."

"Vacation?" said the other. "What about me? We were on our honeymoon!"

The series that redefines the meaning of the word "*gross*"!

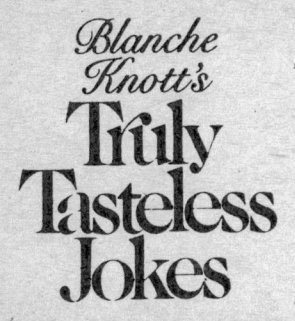

Blanche Knott's Truly Tasteless Jokes

Over 4 million copies of *Truly Tasteless Jokes* in print!

TRULY TASTELESS JOKES IV
_____ 92555-7 $3.95 U.S. _____ $4.95 Can.

TRULY TASTELESS JOKES V
_____ 92556-5 $3.95 U.S. _____ $4.95 Can.

TRULY TASTELESS JOKES VI
_____ 92130-6 $3.95 U.S. _____ 92131-4 $4.50 Can.

TRULY TASTELESS JOKES VII
_____ 92785-1 $3.99 U.S. _____ $4.99 Can.

TRULY TASTELESS JOKES VIII
_____ 92557-3 $3.95 U.S. _____ $4.95 Can.

TRULY TASTELESS JOKES IX
_____ 92611-1 $3.95 U.S. _____ $4.95 Can.

TRULY TASTELESS JOKES X
_____ 92344-9 $3.50 U.S. _____ $4.50 Can.

Publishers Book and Audio Mailing Service
P.O. Box 120159, Staten Island, NY 10312-0004
Please send me the book(s) I have checked above. I am enclosing $ _____ (please add $1.50 for the first book, and $.50 for each additional book to cover postage and handling. Send check or money order only—no CODs) or charge my VISA, MASTERCARD or AMERICAN EXPRESS card.

Card number _____

Expiration date _____ Signature _____

Name _____

Address _____

City _____ State/Zip _____
Please allow six weeks for delivery. Prices subject to change without notice. Payment in U.S. funds only. New York residents add applicable sales tax.

READ MY LIPS.

The Wit & Wisdom of GEORGE BUSH

With some reflections by Dan Quayle
edited by Ken Brady & Jeremy Solomon

THE WIT & WISDOM OF GEORGE BUSH
Brady & Solomon, eds.
_____ 91687-6 $2.95 U.S.   _____ 91688-4 $3.95 Can.

Publishers Book and Audio Mailing Service
P.O. Box 120159, Staten Island, NY 10312-0004
Please send me the book(s) I have checked above. I am enclosing $ _____ (please add $1.50 for the first book, and $.50 for each additional book to cover postage and handling. Send check or money order only—no CODs) or charge my VISA, MASTERCARD or AMERICAN EXPRESS card.

Card number _____
Expiration date _____ Signature _____
Name _____
Address _____
City _____ State/Zip _____
Please allow six weeks for delivery. Prices subject to change without notice. Payment in U.S. funds only. New York residents add applicable sales tax.

BUSH 9/89

❈ HERE'S HOW ❈

HOW TO BUY A CAR by James R. Ross
The essential guide that gives you the edge in buying a new or used car.
_____ 90198-4 $3.95 U.S. _____ 90199-2 $4.95 Can.

THE WHOLESALE-BY-MAIL CATALOG—UPDATE 1986 by The Print Project
Everything you need at 30% to 90% off retail prices—by mail or phone!
_____ 90379-0 $3.95 U.S. _____ 90380-4 $4.95 Can.

TAKING CARE OF CLOTHES: An Owner's Manual for Care, Repair and Spot Removal by Mablen Jones
The most comprehensive handbook of its kind...save money—and save your wardrobe!
_____ 90355-3 $4.95 U.S. _____ 90356-1 $5.95 Can.

AND THE LUCKY WINNER IS...The Complete Guide to Winning Sweepstakes & Contests by Carolyn and Roger Tyndall with Tad Tyndall
Increase the odds in your favor—all you need to know.
_____ 90025-2 $3.95 U.S. _____ 90026-0 $4.95 Can.

THE OFFICIAL HARVARD STUDENT AGENCIES BARTENDING COURSE
The new complete guide to drinkmaking—the $40 course now a paperback book!
_____ 90427-4 $3.95 U.S. _____ 90430-4 $4.95 Can.

Publishers Book and Audio Mailing Service
P.O. Box 120159, Staten Island, NY 10312-0004
Please send me the book(s) I have checked above. I am enclosing $ _____ (please add $1.50 for the first book, and $.50 for each additional book to cover postage and handling. Send check or money order only—no CODs) or charge my VISA, MASTERCARD or AMERICAN EXPRESS card.

Card number _____

Expiration date _____ Signature _____

Name _____

Address _____

City _____ State/Zip _____

Please allow six weeks for delivery. Prices subject to change without notice. Payment in U.S. funds only. New York residents add applicable sales tax.